Meet Cedric Dean

AUTHOR | MOTIVATIONAL SPEAKER | EDUCATOR

CEDRIC LAMONTE DEAN (born June 14, 1972) is an American author, activist, and educator. He is perhaps best known for writing "How to Stop the Killing," "How to Save Our Children from Crime Drugs and Violence," and "How to Stop Your Children from Going to Prison." Dean is founder of Safeguard Atone Validate Educate (SAVE), which is a national morality-centered movement dedicated to preventing lawlessness and building character in misguided minds, and Save a Child Month, an annual (New Year) initiative to make young people job-ready instead of jail-ready.

CONTENTS

EARLY LIFE AND BACKGROUND

Cedric Dean was born in Charlotte, N.C., to a single-parent Christian mother.

At 13-years-old, Dean was re-birthed into a new world of crime, drugs, guns, and violence. He had a short-lived stint as an armed robber of drug dealers. When he was sixteen, he was charged and convicted of robbery with a dangerous weapon, and he spent five and a half years in prison.

Eleven months after his release in February 1994, Dean was charged in a six count federal indictment for Conspiracy to Distribute Crack Cocaine and possession of a firearm by a convicted felon. He was convicted of the charges May 20, 1996 and sentenced to Life plus five years.

AUTHOR

Seven years into his second prison term, Dean was placed in a Special Housing Unit, where he was confined in a cell for 23 hours a day. With a lot of free time on his hands, he read an urban street novel entitled: "B-More-Careful" by Shannon Holmes, who had also served time in prison. He enjoyed the book so much that, upon completion of reading it, he started writing a tale of his own: "For the Love of the Streets," Dean's first literary work, which was published in 2008.

"Mine is the tale of someone whose faith in God, willingness to change, strength, and infatuation to overcome barriers, impediments, and unusual odds can be a blueprint for anyone on the path of (premature) death and self-destruction," Dean wrote in "How to Save Our Children from Crime Drugs and Violence," a self-help book published in 2010. "Cedric Dean has himself crossed over the threshold of crime and violence to become the advocate for responsive change in our youth," said author Eugene Linwood, founder of 'Reaching Out Beyond Bars.' "I have proudly watched him mentor, teach and apply tough love to redirect the pain, fear and uncertainness of young prisoners into courage, dedication and commitment. Cedric has done what many people have tried to do with our youth but you must walk the walk and talk the talk."

When Dean entered the literary arena in 2002, he had very little to look forward to, serving Life without parole. He read books on writing and studied the styles of established writers. He first enrolled in an inmate-taught Creative Writing Class. He completed that and went on to eventually teach a writing course of his own. "I was also not supposed to become a teacher and transform gangsters into gentlemen inside of prisons," Dean wrote, "but I made a promise to the people who helped me along the way that I would help others who are living like I used to live. I didn't think it was possible for someone with a past like mine to be given the opportunity to teach anyone anything." It was. And Dean's teachings have helped hundreds of prisoners obtain their General Education Diploma and thousands more change their lives for the better. "His ability to focus his energy in a positive way has set an excellent example for many of the younger inmates who look to him as a leader," Lance Cole, a Federal Bureau of Prisons Supervisor of Education, said about "Dean's infectious energy and enthusiasm."

SOCIAL REFORMER IN PRISON

Around 2004 aged 32 Dean took a teaching job at the United States Penitentiary (USP) in Coleman, Florida. This assignment was pivotal: it introduced him to character education methods, to psychoanalysis, to activism (he served as the executive director of NAACP Prison Branch 5135), and also to taking direct action to bring about social change. The work and experience with the NAACP were without question very significant in the development of Cedric's own ideas and direction, and all from a low-profiled teaching appointment.

Cedric's early specialization was prisoner analysis, in which his interest and research expanded following his transfer to USP Atwater (in California) in 2005, where he also engaged in activist work and teaching GED, and later life skills.

Cedric's early work focused primarily on testing and extending Gandhi's theory in relation to the effect of Truth and Love as supreme values of human psychology, with a strong emphasis on how society affects childhood maturation. This research entailed detailed social activism and awakened him to the doctrine of non-violence and love, notably conducted in early 2006 with grieving gang members of the CRIPS, whose infamous co-founder, Stanley "Tookie" Williams, had been executed. These experiences especially helped Cedric to realize that Gandhi's ideas lacked vital urban criminal dimensions, and provided a key for his 'biopsychoactive' perspective.

Cedric subsequently moved to four other United States Penitentiaries, continuing his focus on prisoner welfare, and eventually expanding his concentration to child welfare, and also created Save a Child Month in 2012 to address juvenile delinquency, treat trauma and mental illness. When the Sandy Hook Elementary School shooting devastated America, Cedric provided some key solutions to the surge in gun violence in his book: "How to Stop the Killing," which he released on the one-year anniversary

(December 14, 2013). He was awarded a lesser security transfer, but he continued his research and writing, leading the largest prisoner-led movement in America - Safeguard Atone Validate Educate.

COMMUNITY ACTIVIST

In 2009, Dean founded Safeguard Atone Validate Educate with the objective of helping all young people with academic, behavior, and financial problems graduate from high school and become more employable. One year later, in 2010, he received the Federal Bureau of Prisons' highest award: Call-to-Service Award - becoming the first United States Penitentiary Lee inmate to receive such an honor. He was known throughout the prison as "A Leader's Leader."

In late 2010, Dean reached for wider outreach by recording the first in a series of motivational speech presentations for the international media. "Here is a young man who is doing stuff out of prison that we are not even doing in our communities," said Janice Peak-Graham, radio host of 'Our Common Ground.' "We need 10 Cedric's in the community on the outside." He conducted online motivational counseling sessions not only for at-risk youth but also for the parents and teachers of at-risk youth. "This urgent call to action for each of us and for our Country is to work with one another and government officials in our communities to find ways to make our communities safer and to foster positive relationships with our children," Dean said in his "I have A Plan" speech. "My plan will SAVE - safeguard, atone, validate, and educate our children. With this plan we will be able to teach our children how to live side-by-side and deal with their differences without malice or violence. With this plan we will take major steps to substitute the pipeline to prison with a pipeline to prosperity for many of our children."

BOOKS

Dean details his life and the relationships that have helped reshape it in his 17 published books. Much more than an average incarcerated author, Dean's life-saving books, which are divided into a series of written exercises in workbooks, focus on areas of peer pressure - such as bullying, anger management, and misguided thinking - as well as on areas of self-worth, such as self-confidence, courage, and character. "I applaud you, even while serving time in prison for stepping up and taking responsibility for helping find a solution," Kevin Jennings, former assistant deputy secretary of education wrote to Dean in 2010.

In 2011, Dean collaborated with the Federal Bureau of Prisons and launched a replica of his SAVE Program called RISE (Rehabilitate Integrate Stimulate Educate). "The hearts, souls, and minds of each of you can rise," Dean wrote in a message to the misguided. "Power is in your ability to use your mind. The more you think, the more powerful you become."

SELF-HELP BOOKS

How to Stop Your Children from Going to Prison (2008)

Leaders Breed Leaders (2009)

How to Save Our Children from Crime Drugs and Violence (2010)

Born Leaders (2011)

How to Stop the Killing (2013)

My Mother, My Best Friend (2018)

NEW LIFE CURRICULUM WORKBOOKS

Controlling Your Thoughts (2011)

Overcoming Peer Pressure (2011)

Anger Management (2011)

Solving Social Problems - Bullying (2011)

New Hope (2011)

ADULT WORKBOOKS

How to Stop Your Children from Going to Prison (2011)

Leaders Breed Leaders (2011)

SAVE's Effective Communication Curriculum (2014)

FICTION

For the Love of the Streets (2008)

Pimping in the Name of the Lord (2008)

Operation Con-Freedom (2008)

5-LEVEL PARADIGM OF PEACE

1. Goodwill - kindness, compassion, sympathy

2. Genuineness - honesty, acceptance, contrition, consideration

3. God-fearing - faithful, trustworthy, devoted, honorable, virtuous

4. Gracefully - balanced, dignified, self-respecting, diplomatic, prudent

5. Gradually - step-by-step, bit-by-bit, forward-looking, ducks in a row

"We must practice each principle simultaneously, emphasizing the third, which deals with the most significant for procurement of peace," Dean said about the 5-level Paradigm of Peace. He gave these examples in use:

"You can't achieve peace when you have goodwill (level 1, but you're not God-fearing (level 3), which represents the CENTER of the five principles....You can be honest (level 2) but you must also be prudent (level 4) in your pursuit for peace."

MILESTONES

1972 - Born Cedric Lamonte Dean in Charlotte, N.C.

1988 - Sentenced to 14 years for robbery with a dangerous weapon

1990 - Earned General Education Diploma

1994 - Released from prison after serving 66 months

1995 - Indicted for a federal drug conspiracy

1996 - Sentenced to Life plus five years

2004 - Appointed Executive Director of NAACP Prison Branch 5135 and became GED and Creative Writing teacher

2005 - Appeared in written word before members of Congressional Black Caucus

2008 - Became first federal prisoner to publish (5) books from prison in 1 year

2009 - Federal judge reduced his sentence to 35 years pursuant to sentencing guideline changes. Dean found Safeguard Atone Validate Educate to combat juvenile delinquency

2010 - Received Teacher's Assistant certification from U.S. Department of Labor

2011 - Became first federal prisoner to receive a Civil Service and a Call-to-Service award

2012 - Founded Save a Child Month, an annual New Year's initiative to dismantle the juvenile pipeline to premature death and imprisonment. Fair Sentencing Act reduced his sentence to 27 years

2013 - Founded SAVE Institute and K-12 Incarceration Prevention Class Curriculum. Published 17th book: How to Stop the Killing

2014 - Developed Psychoactive Theory

2015 – Sentenced reduced to 24 years and 4 months

2017 – November 29, 2017 released from federal prison

2018 – Received a Humanitarian Award

2019 – Attended the State of the Union Address with N.C. Congresswoman Alma Adams

CEDRIC DEAN AT A GLANCE

BIRTH NAME: Cedric Lamonte Dean

BORN: June 14, 1972, in Charlotte, N.C.

AUTHOR: Published his first self-help book: "How to Stop Your Children from Going to Prison," in 2008. Denounced his past criminal lifestyle in 2009. Became first federal prisoner to simultaneously receive a Call-to-Service Award and a Civil Service Award in 2011.

EDUCATOR: Began teaching GED and Adult Continuing Education classes for federal prisoners in 2004. Became a U.S. Department of Labor Teachers apprentice in 2006. Received his Teacher's Assistant certification in 2010, after helping more than 500 federal prisoners obtain their GEDs. Launched an 8-part New Life Curriculum series in mid-2011. Designed a K-12 Incarceration Prevention Class model in 2012. In 2013, Dean founded the SAVE Institute. In 2014, Dean developed his Psychoactive Theory.

ACTIVIST: Appointed Executive Director of NAACP Prison Branch 5135. Founded Safeguard Atone Validate Educate (SAVE) in 2009 and launched Save a Child Month in January 2012. SAVE is a prisoner-led campaign that includes character education, employment preparation, counseling, mentoring and training.

Cedric Dean's Community Activism Snapshot

- Organized Save a Child Program with CMPD Chief Kerr Putney and Sheriff-elect Garry McFadden January 2018
- Received Federal EIN for Non-Profit Organization (Safeguard Atone Validate Educate) January 2018
- Contracted by CMPD Chief Kerr Putney to coordinate the Community Empowerment Initiative in February 2018
- Partnered with Cox Media/WSOC in March 2018
- Assigned to represent CMPD on Commissioner Vilma Leake committee with City Manager, County Manager, CMS Superintendent, and other community leaders in March 2018
- Received waiver from CMS Superintendent Clayton Wilcox to instruct a Character Education Course in March 2018
- Received 501(c)3 status for SAVE April 2018
- Was a campaign strategist for Sherriff-elect Garry McFadden and District Attorney Spencer Merriweather
- Formed a partnership with Radio One and took 20 children to the radio station April 2018
- Formed a partnership with the Carolina School of Broadcasting and took 20 children to the school May 2018
- Partnered with Second Harvest and Hickory Grove Baptist Church to provide FREE groceries for families at Thomasboro Academy June 2018
- Graduated 15 Character Education Development students at Thomasboro Academy June 2018
- Partnered with the Mayor's Mentoring Alliance June 2018
- Partnered with Second Harvest, CMPD, Sheriff-elect Garry McFadden to feed approximately 500 families in the Beattis Ford Road corridor June 2018
- Provided a FREE summer mentoring program from June to August 2018
- Government Initiatives
- Partnered with Northside Baptist Church in July 2018
- Partnered with Restore Global in July 2018
- Partnered with CMPD and the Big 10 Super Event July 2018
- Partnered with the Carolina Panthers for the development of a flag football league July 2018
- Headlined "The Empowerment Authors Showcase" July 17, 2018
- Graduated 22 children from the CMPD-sponsored SAVE Mentoring Program
- Traveled with Sherriff-elect Garry McFadden to Dallas, Texas vetting a technology provider August 2018
- Took 22 children to the Carolina Panthers pre-season game against New England August 2018

- Partnered with Wells Fargo for a Financial Literacy Class for SAVE children at Thomasboro Academy August 2018
- Partnered with West Charlotte High School Entrepreneur class September 2018
- Joined The Securus Foundation October 00002018
- Received a Humanitarian Award from CUC100 November 2018
- Selected to be keynote Speaker at Mayor's Mentoring Alliance 2019 Awards Show in November 2018
- Attended the State of the Union Address with N.C. Congresswoman Alma Adams

Media
- Press releases have been serviced to local, regional and national outlets
- Charlotte Observer. Cover and feature story
- Article in Returning Citizens Magazine
- Interviewed by WSOC and WBTV
- Radio One and Beasley Media Group radio shows
- Social Media Outreach
    - Information on SAVE Program has been posted on Facebook, Instagram, Twitter and Linkedin accounts.

POLICE

CHARLOTTE-MECKLENBURG

Date: 03/16/2018

To: Charlotte-Mecklenburg Schools Superintendent, Dr Clayton Wilcox

From: Chief of Police Kerr Putney

Subject: Volunteer Waiver for Cedric Dean

The Charlotte-Mecklenburg Police Department is currently sponsoring Mr. Cedric Dean to provide youth oriented training in support of the Community Empowerment Initiative. This program is currently being delivered, in conjunction with the Charlotte-Mecklenburg School system, at Martin Luther King, Jr Middle School and Thomasboro Academy. CMPD is aware of Mr. Dean's criminal history, which most recently includes a felony arrest and conviction for an incident in 1995. Mr. Dean currently provides youth-oriented education through the SAVE (Safeguard, Atone, Validate, Educate) program, which seeks to reduce juvenile delinquency and prepare youth for career readiness through education, and to build resiliency against decisions which would lead to criminal justice system involvement. CMPD supports the authorization by CMS for Mr. Dean to provide this CMPD-funded programming at CMS facilities..

AT THE TABLE WITH THE CHARLOTTE CITY MANAGER, MARCUS JONES AND SCHOOL SUPERINTENDENT CLAYTON WILCOX

POLICE

CHARLOTTE-MECKLENBURG
POLICE DEPARTMENT

To whom it may concern:

My name is LeBraun Evans and I serve as the lieutenant over Community Engagement for the Charlotte-Mecklenburg Police Department. I have been a police officer for 25 years. Although I have worked in various areas of the department during my career, this assignment is by far the most rewarding. I get to interact with community members from all over the County and ensure that they have real dialogue on the issues that both separate and bring us together. I also oversee our youth programs that seek to change the image of officers to our youth and to introduce them to law enforcement as a profession once they come of age.

I had the opportunity to meet Cedric Dean at a panel discussion on police community relations hosted by Stephanie Mills. The event was at times contentious and some sought to blame CMPD for the actions of officers in other states. Cedric was very open and honest about his past and his interactions with officers. He sought to have real dialogue on how persons committing crimes should interact with officers that are trying to suppress crime. His message was very powerful.

Our interaction on that day carried over into observing Cedric's work with SAVE, Promise Youth and many other community engagement efforts. I have seen him partnering with Sheriff-elect Garry McFadden and our own Police Chief Kerr Putney. One of my direct reports, Community Liaison Deon Wimbush is assigned to assist Cedric with all of his efforts.

In his weekly reports to me, Deon has highlighted a level of work and commitment to youth and the underserved in this community that is unparalleled. Cedric has been a model to community activism and uplifting youth since he returned to this community. He is always willing to acknowledge his past mistakes and to offer his time and support to those that are attempting to make a better life for themselves. He is always willing to make himself available at any time of the day or night to help someone.

I fully support Cedric Dean in all of his efforts to improve opportunities for youth and this community as a whole.

Sincerely,

LeBraun Evans

Lt LeBraun Evans
Community Engagement
Charlotte-Mecklenburg Police Department

Building Partnerships to Prevent The Next Crime
601 East Trade Street, Charlotte, NC 28208-2940

POLICE

*CHARLOTTE-MECKLENBURG
POLICE DEPARTMENT*

Subject: Cedric Dean

Dear Sir/Ma'am,

I have been working with Cedric Dean and his SAVE program for several months as part of the Charlotte-Mecklenburg Police Department's Community Empowerment Initiative. Mr. Dean has been a strong advocate for the work the CMPD does with youth in our communities, and he provides children and young adults with very candid and sincere information regarding the consequences of their actions. Mr. Dean also works closely with CMPD as a mentor in the Promise Youth Development program, where we meet weekly with young men in middle school and high school, and work to build their resilience, self-reliance, and develop skills so they can believe in themselves. Mr. Dean, because of his life experience, has tremendous credibility when he shares examples or provides insights. It is also impactful to see him working closely with the police because of his previous interactions with the criminal justice system. Mr. Dean continues to be a strong partner in the community outreach efforts that CMPD participates in.

Regards,

MAJ Ryan M. Butler
Charlotte-Mecklenburg Police Department

State of North Carolina
General Court of Justice
Twenty-Sixth Prosecutorial District
MECKLENBURG COUNTY

SPENCER B. MERRIWEATHER III
DISTRICT ATTORNEY

700 EAST TRADE STREET
CHARLOTTE, NC 28202
TELEPHONE: 704-686-0700
FAX: 704-686-0716

October 26, 2018

To Whom It May Concern:

I am writing to offer a character reference for Cedric Dean based on frequent interactions with him over the course of the last year.

Over a little less than eleven months ago, I came to know Cedric Dean after his release from federal prison and not long after I was appointed District Attorney for Mecklenburg County. I initially met Cedric at a community forum, where—after only few weeks removed from prison--- he sought to meet area leaders to determine how he could make an immediate impact on young people. In the weeks that followed, I would come to see Cedric accompanying young men as they learned how to dress for the workplace, as they discussed police-community relations, and as they learned about our political process. Cedric developed a plan to start his own program for young people called SAVE (Safeguard, Atone, Validate, Educate), where he sought to offer kids from some of Mecklenburg County's most challenged neighborhoods the type of direction and structure so many of them seemed to lack. Where many have talked about developing sustainable programming for youth, Cedric actually delivered. I observed him building trusting relationships with leaders in criminal justice, education, media, and the clergy, with a singular focus of designing a program that both nurtured and provided accountability for our juvenile population. Within six months, Cedric successfully executed his vision, yielding a successful summer program that served scores of children.

In my time as a prosecutor, I have seen many people return from prison and have significant difficulty figuring out how to make meaningful contributions to their community. Cedric has accomplished his reentry with comparably remarkable ease. Cedric's drive, talent, and commitment to do good work has been immediately apparent to all those he encounters. He has done so much to become an engaged citizen, becoming consistently active in political discussions and campaigns. He readily admits mistakes he has made in his past, but he has displayed a strong desire to intercede on behalf of our community's children to divert them away from criminal behavior. In so many ways, Cedric has proven himself to be an asset to this community, and I am proud to attest to the high character he has exhibited in the time since I have known him.

Please feel free to contact me if you would like to discuss this reference further.

Sincerely,

Spencer B. Merriweather III
District Attorney
26th Prosecutorial District of North Carolina

PRISON ACTIVISM

REGISTER NO: 11907-058   NAME..: DEAN   FUNC: PRT
FORMAT.....: TRANSCRIPT   RSP OF: ELK-ELKTON FCI

-------------------------- EDUCATION INFORMATION ----------------------------
FACL ASSIGNMENT DESCRIPTION   START DATE/TIME STOP DATE/TIME
ELK ESL HAS   ENGLISH PROFICIENT   07-09-1997 1335 CURRENT
ELK GED HAS   COMPLETED GED OR HS DIPLOMA   08-06-1997 1122 CURRENT

--------------------------- EDUCATION COURSES -------------------------------
SUB-FACL	DESCRIPTION	START DATE	STOP DATE	EVNT	AC	LV	HRS
ELK	WRITING/PERFORMING COMEDY	06-11-2017	CURRENT				
ELK	WHY INTELLIGENT MINDS MATTER	06-01-2017	CURRENT				
ELK	INVESTING IN REAL ESTATE	06-01-2017	CURRENT				
ELK	CREATING A RELEASE PLAN	06-01-2017	CURRENT				
ELK	ACE: LEADERSHIP	01-24-2017	06-06-2017	P	C	P	16
ELK	ACE: HOW TO START A NON-PROFIT	01-24-2017	06-06-2017	P	C	P	16
ELK	FROM GOOD TO GREAT BUSINESS	01-22-2017	06-06-2017	P	C	P	16
ELK	BUSINESS START UP, SUNDAYS	08-14-2016	01-13-2017	P	C	P	16
ELK	FROM GOOD TO GREAT BUSINESS	08-14-2016	01-13-2017	P	C	P	16
ELK	TOOLS FOR TALKING	08-19-2016	01-13-2017	P	C	P	16
ELK	AIDS AWARENESS-RPP<HN>	06-09-2016	06-09-2016	P	C	P	1
RBK	0730 BUSINESS WORD 1	10-07-2015	06-15-2016	P	W	I	130
RBK	INFORMATIONAL JOB FAIR	04-24-2016	04-30-2016	P	C	P	22
RBK	SCENE WRITING	03-21-2016	05-03-2016	P	C	P	15
RBK	AVP FACILITATORS	03-04-2016	04-15-2016	P	C	P	22
RBK	DEFY VENTURES,CEO OF YOUR LIFE	01-08-2016	03-09-2016	P	W	V	36
RBK	AVP BASIC	12-04-2015	12-07-2015	P	C	P	22
RBK	AVP ADVANCED	01-22-2016	01-24-2016	P	C	P	22
RBK	THINK LIKE AN EDITOR	08-25-2015	10-01-2015	P	C	P	10
RBK	COMPOSING CHILDRENS BOOKS	06-11-2015	08-14-2015	P	C	P	18
RBK	USE GRAMMAR-PUNCTATION-SYNTAX	03-26-2015	05-08-2015	P	C	P	12
RBK	ADVANCED MEMOIR WRITING	01-08-2015	02-26-2015	P	C	P	20
RBK	SMALL BUSINESS ADMINISTRATION	01-12-2015	02-02-2015	P	C	P	6
RBK	HOW TO START A NON-PROFIT ORG	11-04-2014	12-04-2014	P	C	P	12
RBK	MEMOIR WRITING	08-14-2014	10-16-2014	P	C	P	14
RBK	7 HABITS OF EFFECTIVE PEOPLE	06-24-2014	07-30-2014	P	W	V	4
POM	CAR BUYING TIPS AND SKILLS	04-01-2014	05-17-2014	P	C	P	4
POM	CREDIT AND LOANS SHU PRE-REL	04-01-2014	04-20-2014	P	C	P	4
POM	RPP6 ETIQUETTE ACE CLASS	11-17-2013	02-20-2014	P	C	P	12
POM	COMMUNICATION SKILLS ACE	11-14-2013	02-20-2014	P	C	P	6
POM	COUNSELOR GROUP INSIDE OUT	11-06-2013	02-24-2014	P	C	P	12
POM	CREATIVE AND JOURNAL WRITING	08-02-2013	08-09-2013	P	C	P	4
POM	MAKE YOUR MONEY GROW	08-02-2013	08-09-2013	P	C	P	4
POM	JOB SKILL SHU PRE-RELEASE	07-20-2013	07-27-2013	P	C	P	4
POM	LIFE SKILLS SHU PRE-RELEASE	07-20-2013	07-27-2013	P	C	P	4
POM	BEGINNING SPANISH SHU ACE	07-13-2013	07-19-2013	P	C	P	4
POM	CONSUMER SHU PRE-RELEASE CLASS	06-29-2013	07-12-2013	P	C	P	4
POM	PLAYBOOK FOR LIFE	06-29-2013	07-12-2013	P	C	P	4
POM	FORKLIFT OPERATING/SHU ACE	06-29-2013	07-12-2013	P	C	P	4
POM	CAREER PLANNING SHU PRE-REL	06-16-2013	06-28-2013	P	C	P	4

G0002   MORE PAGES TO FOLLOW . . .

"AUTHORIZED BY THE ACT OF JULY 27. 1955
TO ADMINISTER OATHS (18 USC 4004)."

_____
CORRECTIONAL TREATMENT SPECIALIST

6 24-17
_____
DATE

REGISTER NO: 11907-058   NAME..: DEAN   FUNC: PRT
FORMAT.....: TRANSCRIPT   RSP OF: ELK-ELKTON FCI

```
---------------------------- EDUCATION COURSES -----------------------------
SUB-FACL   DESCRIPTION                  START DATE  STOP DATE  EVNT AC LV  HRS
POM        APP/RESUME INTV. SHU PRE-REL 06-16-2013 06-28-2013  P   C  P     4
POM        COMMER.DRIVERS LIC/SHU PART 2 06-08-2013 06-15-2013 P   C  P     4
POM        COMMER.DRIVERS LIC/SHU PART 1 06-08-2013 06-15-2013 P   C  P     4
POM        FINANCIAL PLAN SHU PRE-RELEASE 05-18-2013 05-24-2013 P  C  P     4
POM        EMPLOYMENT SHU PRE-RELEASE   05-18-2013 05-24-2013  P   C  P     4
POM        CREDIT AND LOANS SHU PRE-REL 05-18-2013 05-24-2013  P   C  P     4
POM        INVESTING/INSUR SHU PRE-REL  05-04-2013 05-10-2013  P   C  P     4
POM        ANGER MANAGEMENT SHU PRE-REL 04-27-2013 05-03-2013  P   C  P     4
POM        CHECKING/SAVING/ATM SHU      04-27-2013 05-03-2013  P   C  P     4
BTF GP     RP-PARENTING;T-F830-1030AM   01-25-2012 03-13-2012  P   C  P    20
BTF GP     ACE-START NON PROFIT;T630-830 02-02-2012 03-13-2012 P  C  P    20
BTF GP     ACE-START LEGITIMATE BUS;630-8 01-25-2012 03-13-2012 P C  P    20
BTF GP     ACE-FUNDING SM BUS;R630-830PM 09-12-2011 11-07-2011 P  C  P    20
BTF GP     ACE TEACH TUTORS M,TH 230-330 08-01-2011 08-26-2011 P  C  P    20
BTF GP     ACE-PERFORMING ARTS;T;230-330 07-05-2011 07-29-2011 P  C  P    20
BTF GP     RP-PARENTING;M-6:30-8:30 PM  06-08-2011 07-19-2011  P   C  P    20
BTF GP     TRANSITIONS INMATE MENTOR PROG 05-02-2011 07-01-2011 P C  P    32
BTF GP     ACE-EFFECTIVE COMM;W630-830PM 06-08-2011 07-26-2011 P  C  P    20
BTF GP     ACE-HOW TO WRITE BOOK;R630-830 06-08-2011 07-26-2011 P C  P    20
BTF GP     ACE-LEADERSHIP;T630-830PM    06-08-2011 07-20-2011  P   C  P    20
LEE        TRAINING FOR LITERACY TUTORS 04-08-2010 05-19-2011  P   W  I   480
LEE        USP ACE - THE MUSIC INDUSTRY 01-31-2011 03-16-2011  P   C  P    10
LEE        EFFECTIVE COMMUNICATION BASICS 01-31-2011 03-16-2011 P C  P    10
LEE        HOW TO WRITE & GET PUBLISHED 01-31-2011 03-16-2011  P   C  P    10
LEE        STARTING/OWNING NONPROFIT    01-31-2011 03-16-2011  P   C  P    10
LEE        BASICS OF TEACHING           01-31-2011 03-16-2011  P   C  P    10
LEE        RP6 LITERACY IN THE FAMILY   11-19-2010 12-22-2010  P   C  P     4
LEE        GETTING READY TO GET OUT     09-15-2010 11-16-2010  P   C  P    10
LEE        LIFESKILLS AND DEVELOPMENT   09-15-2010 11-16-2010  P   C  P    10
LEE        TEACHERS ASSISTANT APPRENTICE 03-31-2010 11-15-2010 P  C  A  4000
LEE        INCREASING MOTIVATION        09-10-2010 11-10-2010  P   C  P    10
LEE        COMPUTER APPLICATIONS MECC AOE 05-27-2010 09-16-2010 P C  C   240
LEE        SPORTS OFFICIAL CERTIFICATION 05-18-2010 05-27-2010 P  C  P     6
LEE        SELF AWARENESS 1             04-25-2010 07-06-2010 .P   C  P    16
LEE        LEADERS BREED LEADERS WORKSHOP 04-19-2010 04-19-2010 P C  P     3
LEE        RPP5 RPP ORIENTATION         03-18-2010 03-18-2010  P   C  P     1
LEE        RPP1 AIDS AWARENESS          03-18-2010 03-18-2010  P   C  P     1
BSY        YSF, JOB SKILLS SURVEY       11-03-2008 11-03-2008  P   C  P     8
BSY        ELL ORIENTATION              10-30-2008 10-30-2008  P   C  P     1
BSY        COMP LEARNING CENTER ORIEN   10-31-2008 10-31-2008  P   C  P     1
TCP        IC3 CERTIFICATION (COMPUTERS) 07-23-2008 08-01-2008 P  W  V     4
TCP        COMPUTING FUNDIMENTALS       07-23-2008 08-01-2008  C   W  V     0
TCP        EMPLOYMENT RESOURCE CENTER 2 05-07-2008 05-21-2008  P   C  P     9
TCP        AB & CORE STRENGTH EXERCISES 02-14-2008 05-08-2008  P   C  P     9
TCP        EMPLYMENT RESOURCE CENTER USP 03-26-2008 05-07-2008 P  C  P     3
```

G0002   MORE PAGES TO FOLLOW . . .

```
REGISTER NO: 11907-058     NAME..: DEAN                 FUNC: PRT
FORMAT.....: TRANSCRIPT     RSP OF: ELK-ELKTON FCI
```

```
------------------------------ EDUCATION COURSES ------------------------------
SUB-FACL  DESCRIPTION                   START DATE STOP DATE EVNT AC LV  HRS
TCP       USP CERTIFYING UMPIRE CLASS   05-09-2007 05-11-2007  P  C  P    6
ATW       VT OFFICE AUTOMATION          09-15-2006 12-22-2006  P  C  M  108
ATW       WRITING FOR MANUSCRIPTS       07-13-2006 09-23-2006  P  C  P   40
ATW       ACE LIFE SKILLS PREP          07-10-2006 09-23-2006  P  C  P   20
ATW       WRITING FOR MANUSCRIPTS       03-26-2006 06-24-2006  P  C  P   20
ATW       ACE LIFE SKILLS PREP          01-15-2006 03-26-2006  P  C  P   20
ATW       WRITING FOR MANUSCRIPTS       01-15-2006 03-26-2006  P  C  P   20
ATW       BASKETBALL OFFICIAL WEST      02-27-2006 03-17-2006  P  C  P    9
COP       RPP5 RELEASE REQUIREMENT CLASS 09-29-2005 09-29-2005 P  C  P    1
COP       BEG AEORBICS M/W/F 1830-1930  04-13-2005 06-20-2005  P  C  P    3
COP       ACE REAL ESTATE - TUES/THURS  03-24-2004 05-24-2004  P  C  P   16
COP       NESS PLAN ACE CLASS M 6:30-7:3 11-17-2003 02-17-2004 P  C  P   16
COP       FLOOR AEROBICS                07-31-2003 09-29-2003  P  C  P   24
COP       ACE CREATE WRITE M/W 1830-1930 03-13-2003 07-10-2003 P  C  P   26
COP       REFEREE CLINIC                04-09-2003 04-12-2003  P  C  P    4
ATL       BASIC BARBERING, NON-CERT 550H 03-22-2001 06-22-2001 P  C  M  200
ATL       SPORTS OFFICIAL TRAINING      10-06-2000 11-03-2000  P  C  P   10
ATL       CCC/HEALTH AWARENESS          09-08-2000 12-31-2000  P  C  P    8
ATL       INTER SPANISH T&TH 7-8PM,10WKS 01-11-2000 03-29-2000 P  W  I   18
ATL       BEGIN SPAN 7-8 M-W, 10 WKS    08-30-1999 11-22-1999  P  C  P   21
ATL       INTO TO TYPING-COVINGTON-1230 10-26-1999 11-09-1999  P  W  V    3
ATL       BASIC BARBERING M-F 12-7:30 P 05-03-1999 08-10-1999  P  W  I 1300
ATL       BASIC BARBERING M-F 12-7:30 P 11-05-1997 07-16-1998  P  W  I  700
ATL       CARDIOVASCULAR ENDURANCE      09-07-1997 09-15-1997  P  C  P    2
```

CORRECTIONAL TREATMENT SPECIALIST

6-24-17

DATE

```
G0000      TRANSACTION SUCCESSFULLY COMPLETED
```

U. S. Department of Justice

Federal Bureau of Prisons

Federal Correctional Complex

Office of the Lieutenant's   Tucson, Arizona

March 14, 2008

MEMORANDUM FOR WHOM IT MAY CONCERN

FROM: N. Pea, Lieutenant

SUBJECT: Inmate Cedric Dean, #11907-058

This memorandum is written on behalf of the above-mentioned inmate and his work ethic while assigned to the United States Penitentiary, Tucson. Inmate Dean is very cooperative with staff and does a great job keeping the peace amongst the inmates from the Southern Region. He is a very respectful inmate and has been a great asset to the Correctional Services Department. Currently he is working in the Officer Dinning Hall, which is a detail only privileged inmates are permitted to be assigned. Again, this inmate is very cooperative with staff and is willing to help staff at any giving time.

U.S. Department of Justice

Federal Bureau of Prisons

Federal Correctional Complex

Office of the Warden   Tucson, Arizona 85706

February 17, 2008

MEMORANDUM FOR   To Whom it may Concern

FROM: M. Tolin, Recreation Specialist

SUBJECT: Inmate Cedric Dean, #11907-058

Inmate Dean is currently the Basketball Commissioner for the
Intramural Sports league at the USP. He is very organized and
dependable. Prior to the league's activation, inmate Dean taught a
month long Basketball Officials Class. Which consisted of one on
one instruction with each student/referee. Under his management,
there hasn't been and physical confrontations among the inmate
participants. Inmate Dean has remarkable communication skills,
which allows him to prevent smaller problems from becoming larger
problems.

U.S. Department of Justice

Federal Bureau of Prisons

United States Penitentiary, Lee County

P.O. Box 900, Jonesville, Virginia 24263-0900

November 17, 2010

MEMORANDUM FOR WHOM IT MAY CONCERN

FROM: Leigh Anna Collins   *A. Collins*
           Correctional Counselor

SUBJECT: Inmate Cedric Dean #11907-058

This memorandum is written on behalf of the above-mentioned inmate and his work ethics while assigned to USP Lee, Jonesville, VA. Inmate Dean has not received any incident reports while at USP Lee. He has participated actively in educational programs throughout his incarceration and does not have any financial obligations. He has demonstrated a good overall level of responsibility, and he communicates well with staff and other inmates. Inmate Dean has taken on extra work responsibilities in the unit with sanitation without any hesitation. He has helped other inmates in the unit with GED preparation, basic reading skills, and mentoring young inmates to help them with their adjustment with the prison environment.

U.S. Department of Justice

Federal Bureau of Prisons

United States Penitentiary, Lee
P.O. Box 900 Jonesville, Virginia 24263-0900

November 11, 2010

To Whom It May Concern,

I am writing in regards to the contributions of Cedric Dean, Reg. No. 11907-058, to Education programs since his arrival at USP Lee in March, 2010. Dean immediately sought me out to express his interest in developing a series of classes and programs designed to have a positive impact on the other inmates in this institution, as well as people in the community. He began tutoring GED students during the day and several nights each week, helping them prepare for the Official GED Exam. At the same time, he developed a Writer's Workshop course he began teaching in April, 2010.

This past spring, Dean teamed with another inmate to present a one day leadership seminar entitled "Leaders Breed Leaders." This seminar met with such a large response from the population that it had to be presented on three separate occasions. In August, this seminar was presented again, this time in the institution's chapel to an audience of over 130 staff and inmates. This fall, he has volunteered to teach a variety of evening classes, including Leadership, Self Awareness, and Motivational Speaking.

In addition to teaching or leading programs, Dean has taken and completed several classes including, Microsoft Office 2007, a Teacher's Assistant Apprenticeship program certified through the Department of Labor, Training for Literacy Tutors, Self Awareness and Motivation.

Dean's infectious energy and enthusiasm has had a very positive impact on the programs and activities offered at USP Lee. His ability to focus his energy in a positive way has set an excellent example for many of the younger inmates who look to him as a leader. Through his words and his actions, he has demonstrated a strong commitment not only to personal improvement, but also to the betterment of the people in his immediate community, and the community beyond these walls.

Lance Cole
Supervisor of Education
USP LEE
PO Box 900
Jonesville, VA   24263
276-546-0150, Ext. 1119

USP LEE Education Department

Honors

Cedric Dean

For having exemplified leadership and dedication to teaching and mentoring the inmate population.

Call to Service Award

Awarded this 29th day of March 2011

_____
L. Cole, Supervisor Education

_____
H. Chain, Associate Warden

_____
C. Zych, Warden

USP LEE Education Department

Honors

Cedric Dean

For having exemplified commitment to principles of humanitarianism and compassion for the inmate population through Unity in Motion.

Civil Service Award

Awarded this 29th day of March 2011

_____
C. Martin, Teacher

_____
L. Cole, Supervisor of Education

Commonwealth of Virginia

Certificate of Completion of Apprenticeship

Know Ye that **Cedric Dean**

has satisfactorily completed an apprenticeship of 4000 hours at the trade of

Teacher Assistant

on this Tenth day of December 2010 in accordance with the standards approved by the

Virginia Apprenticeship Council and is, by virtue of the statutes of the Commonwealth, awarded this certificate.

In Testimony whereof the official signature of the Virginia Apprenticeship

Council has been subscribed hereon this Third day of January 2011.

Courtney M. Malveaux

Secretary, Virginia Apprenticeship Council

TRANSITIONS INMATE MENTORING PROGRAM

THIS CERTIFIES THAT

CEDRIC DEAN

has successfully completed the TIMP course of study along with the introspection necessary for personal growth and character development. He is therefore awarded this

CERTIFICATE OF ACHIEVEMENT

GIVEN THIS 1ST DAY OF JULY 2011

WARDEN D. R. STEPHENS   TIMP FACILITATOR B. STUBBS

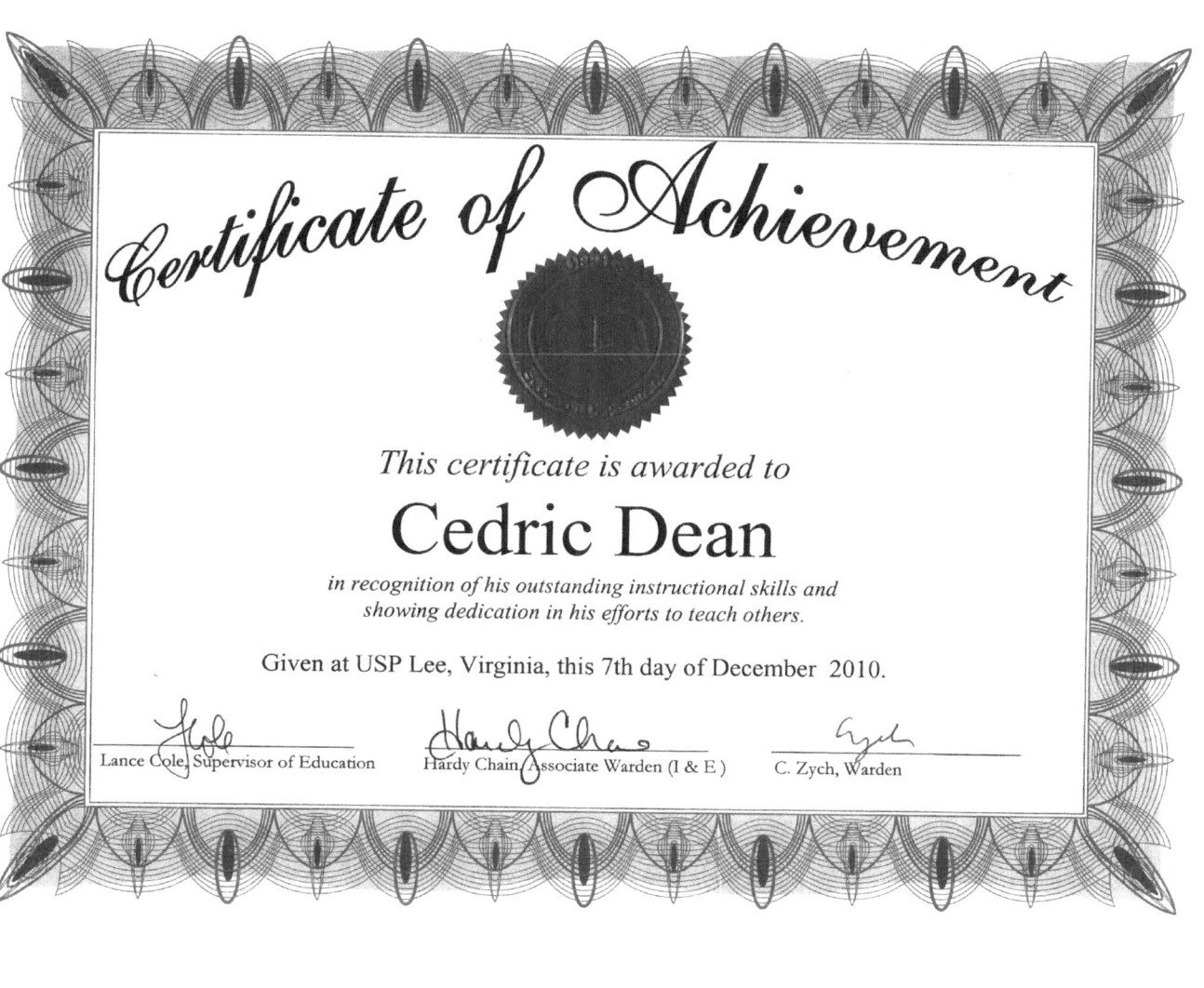

Certificate of Achievement

This certificate is awarded to

Cedric Dean

in recognition of his outstanding instructional skills and showing dedication in his efforts to teach others.

Given at USP Lee, Virginia, this 7th day of December 2010.

Lance Cole, Supervisor of Education

Hardy Chain, Associate Warden (I & E)

C. Zych, Warden

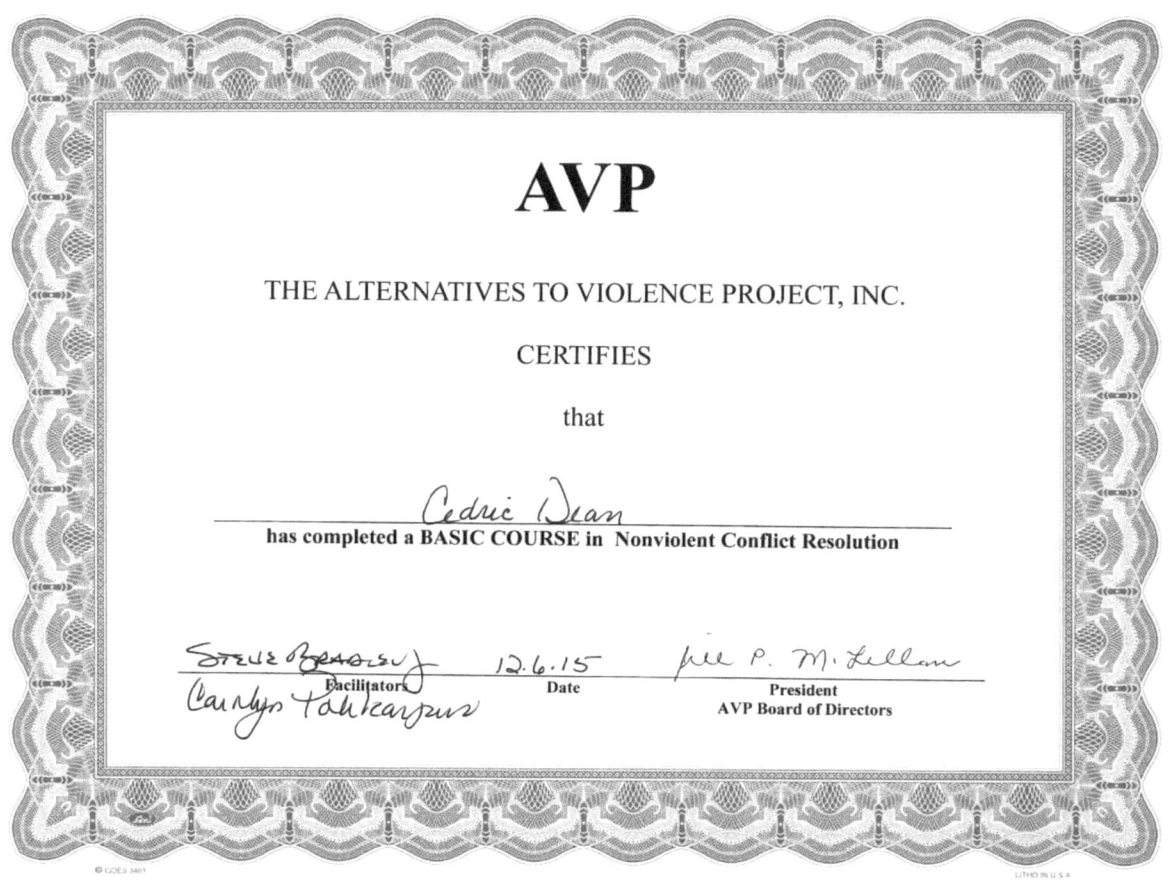

AVP

THE ALTERNATIVES TO VIOLENCE PROJECT, INC.

CERTIFIES

that

Cedric Dean

has completed a BASIC COURSE in Nonviolent Conflict Resolution

Steve Bradley   12.6.15   _Jill P. M. Lellan_

Carolyn Polkarpus

Facilitators   **Date**   **President**
                                            AVP Board of Directors

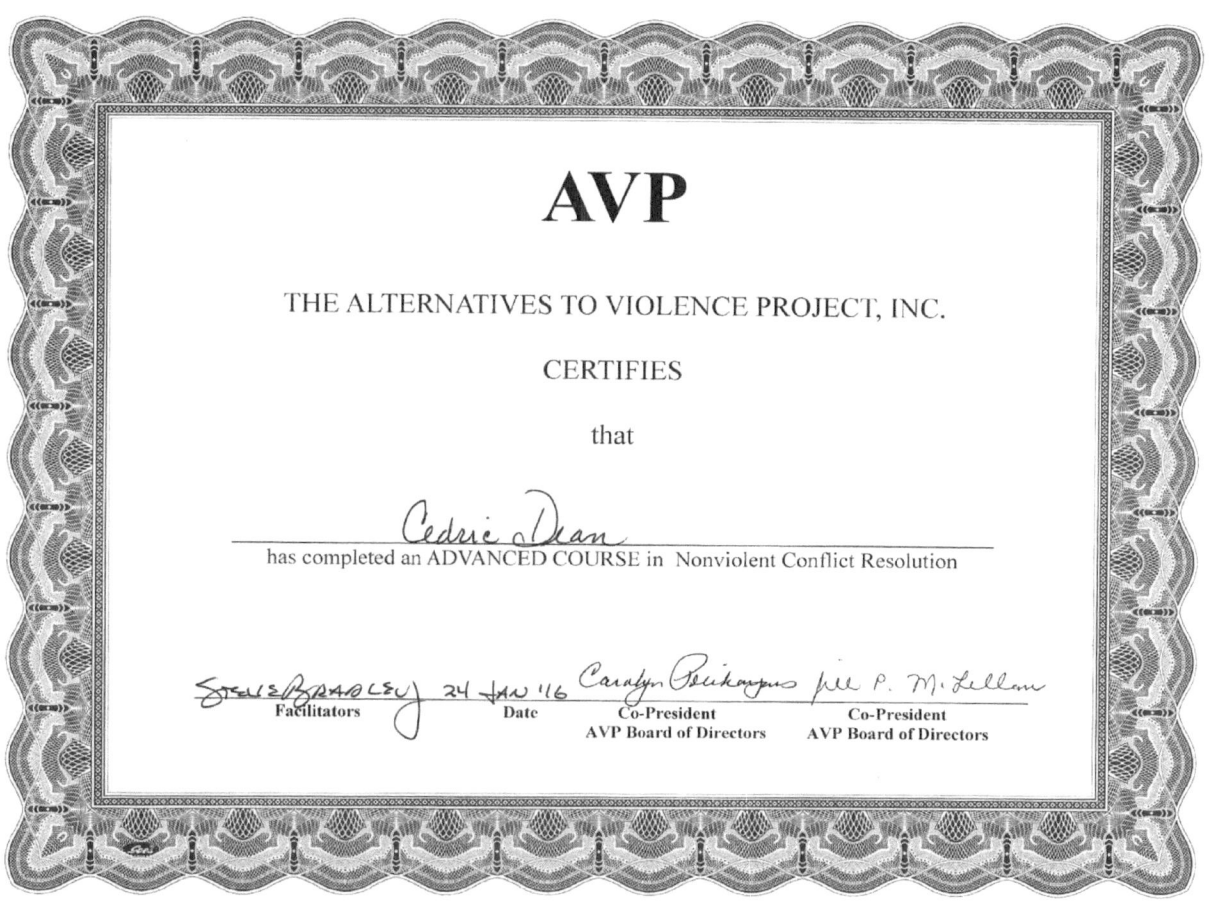

AVP

THE ALTERNATIVES TO VIOLENCE PROJECT, INC.

CERTIFIES

that

Cedric Dean

has completed an ADVANCED COURSE in Nonviolent Conflict Resolution

STEVE BRADLEY	24 JAN '16	Carolyn Reichepus	Jill P. McLellanIII
Facilitators	**Date**	**Co-President**	**Co-President**
		AVP Board of Directors	**AVP Board of Directors**

Date: July 3, 2015

To whom it may concern:

My name is Garry L McFadden, a retired homicide detective from the Charlotte Mecklenburg Police Department who was rehired by the department after 30 years of service. I am currently assigned to the Office of The Chief and work in various roles including community relations. Since my returned in 2011 I have worked in the community with what is commonly known as "at risk kids". Over the past four years have developed many programs and recently recognize by President's Obama Task Force on 21 Century Policing.

I was contacted by Cedric Dean who I have known most of career. While being incarcerated Cedric Dean has written me several times to provide me his focus, which I have seen significantly change over the years. Because of that it is my intention to support the efforts of Cedric Dean immediately upon his release and support his SAVE Program by working very closely with him to save misguided children from premature death and imprisonment. Having worked in Homicide for over two decades and seen lives destroyed by senseless violence first hand, I know "Cedric" could make a difference if provided a chance.

We need more unconventional programs in our community like what "Cedric" is proposing to reach our youth from a different perspective that only someone like him could provide. If given the chance I am sure that Cedric Dean would make a difference and I would strongly encourage him along the way and implement his program in our community efforts.

Thank you and please contact me directly should you wish to verify this letter or have any questions.

Sincerely,

G.L McFadden

Garry L McFadden
Founder/CEO
McFadden Solutions, LLC

MCFADDEN SOLUTIONS

GOGI Education Course Completion Certificate

The recipient of this award is acknowledged for successful completion of a 15-week cycle of the

GOGI LEADERSHIP TRAINING CERTIFICATE PROGRAM, which is a requirement for Peer Coach Certification and facilitation of GOGI studies.

CEDRIC DEAN, #11907-058

October 19, 2017
_____
Date of Issue
Course completion: 10/12/2017

GOGI Founder
Dr. ML "Coach" Taylor

GOGI Education Course
Completion Certificate

The recipient of this award is acknowledged by Getting Out by Going In
(GOGI) for the successful completion of the

GOGI GROUP CERTIFICATE PROGRAM which required daily self-study
and weekly group meetings for 12-15 weeks.

CEDRIC DEAN, #11907-058

October 19, 2017

Date of Issue

Course completion: 10/12/2017

GOGI Founder
Dr. ML "Coach" Taylor

Certificate of Appreciation

awarded to:

Cedric Dean

for volunteering and instructing the
Effective Communication course
at FCI 2 Butner during the Summer Semester 2011.

July 20, 2011
_____
Date

R. Thompson
_____
R. Thompson, Education Specialist

Certificate of Appreciation

awarded to:

Cedric Dean

for volunteering and instructing the
Leadership course
at FCI 2 Butner during the Summer Semester 2011.

July 20, 2011
Date

R. Thompson

R. Thompson, Education Specialist

Certificate of Appreciation

awarded to:

Cedric Dean

for volunteering and instructing the
How To Write and Publish A Book course
at FCI 2 Butner during the Summer Semester 2011.

July 20, 2011
_____
Date

R. Thompson
_____
R. Thompson, Education Specialist

Certificate of Appreciation

awarded to:

Cedric Dean

for volunteering and instructing the
Parenting course
at FCI 2 Butner during the Summer Semester 2011.

July 19, 2011
Date

R. Thompson
R. Thompson, Education Specialist

USP LEE EDUCATION DEPARTMENT

Certificate of Achievement

Cedric Dean

Has satisfactorily completed

Motivational Speaking

Consisting of 16 Hours of Training

This Certificate is hereby issued this 7th day of November, 2010

_____
R. Spears, A.C.E. Coordinator

_____
L. Cole, Supervisor of Education

ଛଠ Certificate of Achievement ଡ଼

Cedric Dean

Has satisfactorily completed

Interpersonal Communication (Life Skills)

Consisting of 10 Hours of Training

This Certificate is hereby issued this 7th day of November, 2010

_____
R. Spears, A.C.E. Coordinator

_____
L. Cole, Supervisor of Education

❧ Certificate of Achievement ❧

Cedric Dean

Has satisfactorily completed

Getting Ready Getting Out

Consisting of 16 Hours of Training

This Certificate is hereby issued this 7th day of November, 2010

_____
R. Spears, A.C.E. Coordinator

_____
L. Cole, Supervisor of Education

Certificate of Completion

This certificate hereby acknowledges

Cedric Dean

for successfully completing each core competency of
Introduction to Non-Profit Organizations,
demonstrating an ongoing commitment to personal
growth and development through continuing education.

Awarded on this 4th day of December, 2014.

Ms. M. Lavigne, *Adult Continuing Education Coordinator*

CHARACTER EDUCATIONAL DEVELOPMENT

PROGRAM

○ Curriculum

RISE: a character educational development program with a four phase curriculum:

- Phase 1 Rehabilitate
  Focuses on providing life skill classes for members of the RISE program

- Phase 2 Integrate
  Focuses on career-related classes

- Phase 3 Stimulate
  Provides self-motivation classes (leadership, communication, and sociology)

- Phase 4 Educate
  Continued education for higher learning (business writing, math, and science)

○ Classroom Materials
Educational materials and workbooks for each student.

SUPPORT

○ Program Optimization Strategy

- On going monthly support

- Program management

- On-call support to help optimize the program

- Troubleshooting based on the needs and/or requests of participants or professionals

Cedric Dean, program creator

Cedric's infectious energy and enthusiasm has had a very positive impact on the program and activities offered. His ability to focus his energy in a positive way has set an excellent example for many who look to him as a leader. Cedric's program enhance participants' principles and morals such as controlling misguided thoughts, anger management, bullying, peer pressure, and refresh basic behavior training. He has also included leadership training to assist in community revitalization.

www.ingramcontent.com/pod-product-compliance
Lightning Source LLC
Chambersburg PA
CBHW06083829O526
45792CB00006BB/1972